Place Your Bets

John Goodwin

Published in association with
The Basic Skills Agency

Hodder Murray

A MEMBER OF THE HODDER HEADLINE GROUP

Orders: please contact Bookpoint Ltd, 130 Milton Park, Abingdon, Oxon OX14 4SB. Telephone: (44) 01235 827720. Fax: (44) 01235 400454. Lines are open from 9.00am to 5.00pm, Monday to Saturday, with a 24-hour message answering service.
Visit our website at www.hoddereducation.co.uk

© John Goodwin 2001, 2006
First published in the Livewire series in 2001 and first published in the Hodder Reading Project series in 2006 by Hodder Murray, an imprint of Hodder Education, a member of the Hodder Headline Group, an Hachette Livre UK Company, 338 Euston Road, London NW1 3BH.

Impression number   10 9 8 7 6 5
Year   2011 2010 2009 2008 2007

Cover photo: Slot machine © Brand X Pictures / Alamy.
Internal artwork © Gary Andrews.
Typeset by Transet Ltd, Coventry, England.
Printed in Great Britain by CPI, Bath.

A catalogue record for this title is available from the British Library

ISBN-13: 978 0 340 91575 2

About the Play

The People

Emma   aged 17
Carla   her sister, aged 15
Mum   their mother

The Scene

Emma and **Carla** have just come home from school.

They are waiting for their mum to come back from work.

Act 1

Carla It isn't there.

Emma Look again.

Carla I have looked again.

Emma Maybe it's hidden under something.

Carla I've looked under everything.

Emma Maybe you took it to Sam's.

Carla I didn't take it to Sam's.

Emma Are you sure?

Carla Emma, my CD player has gone.
We've had a break-in, Emma.

Emma A break-in?

Carla Yes.

Emma We haven't had a break-in.

Carla Then where's the TV gone?

Emma What?

Carla The TV has gone.
Look for yourself.

They go into the kitchen.

Emma Oh yes.

Carla Somebody has broken into the house.
They've nicked my CD player and
the TV.

*Emma is still looking at the space where the TV
used to be.*

Emma No they haven't.

Carla They must have.

Emma Er … no. The TV had to go back to
the shop.

Carla What?

Emma Yeah … it had to go in for repair.

Carla What was wrong with it?

Emma The sound had gone.

Carla It was working perfectly yesterday.

Emma Carla, I am telling you the TV
has gone in for repair OK?

Carla No, it is not OK.

Emma	I can't stand about arguing, Carla.
	I have to get the tea ready.
	Mum will be home soon.
Carla	But what about my CD player?
Emma	I've already said you must have left
	it at Sam's.
	Go round there and check it out.
Carla	It will be a waste of time.
Emma	Carla, just go.

Act 2

Half an hour later.

Mum   My feet are killing me.

Emma   Mum, we need to talk.

Mum   I've been on my feet all day.

Emma   Mum.

Mum   Friday is such a busy day.

Emma   You've been up to your tricks again, haven't you?

Mum   Still it's a nice tea you've made, Emma.

Emma   Don't try and change the subject.

Mum   I'm not changing the subject.

Emma   Where's the TV gone?

Mum   What?

Emma   And Carla's CD player?

Mum	I don't know what you're talking about.
Emma	Yes you do.
	You've been gambling again, haven't you?
Mum	I have not.
Emma	Scratch cards is it?
Mum	No.
Emma	Betting on the horses?
Mum	No.
Emma	How much money did you lose?
Mum	I haven't lost any money.
Emma	Yes you have.
	That's why you sold Carla's CD player and the TV.
Mum	I haven't been gambling.
Emma	How could you?
	Your own daughter's CD player.
Mum	I haven't done anything.
Emma	Yes you have.
	Tell the truth, Mum.
Mum	It's only temporary.

Emma	So you took them down the second-hand shop.
Mum	I needed a bit of cash. I got a good tip on the horses.
Emma	But the horse lost.
Mum	Yes.
Emma	You said you'd never gamble again.
Mum	This was different, Emma.
Emma	You promised me.
Mum	I'll get her CD player back. I'll get the TV back.
Emma	What are you going to use for money?
Mum	I'll get them both back. It'll be easy.
Emma	Oh yeah. Like last time?

Act 3

*Later that night. **Carla** is looking at her CD player.*

Emma So there it is.

Carla Yes.

Emma It was here all the time.

Carla Where did you find it?

Emma In your bedroom.

Carla I looked in my bedroom.

Emma Did you?

Carla Yes.

Emma Well I found it.

Carla What's this scratch on it?

Emma What scratch?

Carla This big scratch here. Look.
There's a bit that's been
smashed off as well.

Emma	It must have always been like that.
Carla	You're a liar, Emma.
Emma	Don't call me a liar.
Carla	You're not telling me the truth.
Emma	What do you mean?
Carla	Something's happened to my CD player. I want to know what you've done to it.
Emma	I've done nothing to it.
Carla	Tell me the truth.
Emma	Right, I will.
Carla	Come on then.
Emma	It's Mum. She sold it down the second-hand shop.
Carla	What?
Emma	For money to go gambling with.
Carla	What are you talking about?
Emma	She's an addict, Carla. Like some people are drug addicts. Mum is a gambling addict.

Carla   She never is.

Emma   Oh yes.

She sold the TV for money
to go gambling with.

Carla   No.

Emma   Oh yes.

Carla   I don't believe you.

Emma   You remember the holiday we were
going on?

Carla   Yeah.

Emma   We didn't go because she spent the
money on betting on the horses.

Carla   Why didn't you tell me?

Emma   She didn't want you to know about
it. I got your CD player back.

Carla   How did you do that?

Emma   With the money I saved from my
Saturday job.

Carla   Emma …

Emma   But I can't do it any more, Carla.

Carla   Where is she?

Emma   She's gone to the pub.
When she gets back we've got to
sort her out.
I can't do it myself.
I need you to help me.
Will you help me?

Act 4

An hour later.

Mum   What's this then?

Emma   We need to talk to you.

             Don't we, Carla?

Carla   Yeah.

Mum   Can't it wait till tomorrow?

Emma   No, it can't.

Mum   But it's late.

             We've all got to be up early in the

             morning.

Emma   It won't take long.

Mum   Go on then if you must.

Emma   Right … well … go on, Carla.

Carla   You say it, Emma.

Emma   But you said you'd start it off.

14

Mum	Come on.
Emma	We want you to give up gambling.
Mum	Is this what all this fuss is about?
Carla	Yeah.
Mum	Look, I've said I've given it up, OK?
Emma	No, Mum. You've said that before.
Mum	Oh come on, Emma,
	I need to get to bed.
Emma	No, Mum. This time it's for real.
	We come home from school,
	the TV and Carla's CD player are
	missing.
Mum	I said it won't happen again.
Emma	How many times have you
	said that?
	I've lost count.
	What will it be next time?
	The kitchen table? Our own beds?
	All our clothes?
	I've lost all my savings
	because of you.
Mum	I said I'm sorry.

Emma   That's not enough.

I worked every Saturday for that cash and now I haven't got a penny.

Mum   I'll pay it back.

Emma   Oh yeah.

Mum   Really I will.

Carla   We've decided, Mum.

Mum   Decided what?

Carla   If you do it again we're going.

Mum   Where would you go to?

Emma   We'd go to Dad's house.

Mum   You wouldn't do that.

Carla   Yes, we would.

Mum   He'd never have you.

Carla   He would.

Emma   So we're telling you straight, Mum.

No second chances.

Carla   We'll be out of here fast.

Emma   So now you know.

It's gambling or us.

You choose.

Act 5

Three weeks later.
Mum enters carrying a big cardboard box.

Mum   Mind out of the way, Carla.
I need to put this down.

Carla   What have you got there?

Mum   Just move.

Mum puts the box down.

Emma   What have you got?

Mum   Go on, Carla, open the box.

Carla opens the box.

Emma   What is it?

Carla   It's a TV.

Mum	It's our TV.
	I got it back from the shop.
Carla	Great!
Emma	Where did you get the money from?
Mum	From my wages. I saved up.
Emma	Right.
Mum	I'll pay you back, Emma.
	Next week.
	I should manage it by
	next week.

Carla takes the TV out of the box and plugs it in.

Carla	Just in time to watch the football.
Mum	Things are sorted.
	Back on the way up.
Carla	Yeah.
Mum	I've given up gambling for good.
Emma	Yeah.

Act 6

Two weeks later.

Mum   There you are, Emma, sixty pounds.

Emma   Really?

Mum   Yes, count it. That's all I owe you.

Emma   Thanks.

Mum   There's a present for you, Carla …
here.

Carla   Great!

Mum   Maybe you could buy yourself a
CD with it.

Carla   Wow! Thirty quid.
I can buy two with this!

Mum   Why not? And I thought we
could go on holiday.
To make up for the one
we missed in the summer.

Emma	You've given me seventy pounds.
Mum	What?
Emma	You owed me sixty.
	But you've given me seventy.
Mum	Well keep it anyway.
Emma	Where did you get all this money from?
Mum	I got a rise at work.
Emma	A rise?
Mum	Yes. A big one.
Emma	Really …
Mum	So where do you fancy for a holiday then, Carla?
Emma	You're a liar, Mum.
Mum	Somewhere on a hot sunny beach, Carla? Soaking up the sun?
Emma	Carla …
Carla	What?
Emma	It's time we were going.
Carla	Going where?
Emma	We need to pack our things.
Carla	What?

Emma   We're going to Dad's.

Carla   What are you on about?

Emma   You've won on the horses haven't you, Mum?

Mum   Of course I haven't.

Emma   There's no way a raise could pay for all this.

You must think we're stupid.

Mum   I never thought that.

I just wanted to give you some good things for once.

Emma   So you went back to gambling.

Mum   I won a thousand pounds.

Carla   How much?

Mum   Look it's all here.

Mum takes a thick bundle of notes out of her pocket.

Carla   I don't believe it.

Mum   I won the jackpot at bingo.

Nobody's won it for three weeks.

It was a roll-over.

Carla	Look at all that cash!
Emma	And now you expect us to roll over.
Mum	It was just one game of bingo.
	It only cost me a couple of quid.
	Where's the harm in that?
Emma	You promised us no more gambling.
Carla	But we can go on holiday, Emma.
Emma	No.
Mum	I won't go again.
Emma	But you will. You will.
	This time you've won.
	But what about next time?
	And the time after that?
	You throw away your life
	on betting.
	On bingo.
	On the lottery.
	On scratch cards.
	On arcade games.
	Well, I'm not going to see you do it.
	I'm going to Dad's.

Mum   No. Please, Emma.

Emma   You can do what you like, Carla,
but I'm going now.

Mum   No, Emma.

Emma ignores her mother.
She goes into her bedroom and begins
to pack her bag.